Huffington
Award-Winning Life Coa

STACIA PIERCE

SUCCESS ATTRACTION NOTES & QUOTES

How to Finally Take Control of Your Life, Your Income and Your Sanity with 30 Days of Simple Actions for Successful Daily Living

Success Attraction Notes and Quotes
30 Days of Insight and Inspiration to Improve Your Life and Increase Your Income

ISBN-13:978-0-9912323-3-8

Table of Contents

Introduction

Congratulations on taking the awesome step of selecting this life-changing book. Over the course of the next 30 days, it will serve as your guide to help you change your life and take you to the next level. Each day, you will be presented with a new Success Note that when acted upon, will empower you to achieve positive change. To reinforce what you learn, each lesson comes complete with a fast-action exercise, journal pages and a powerful affirmation to accelerate your results. Within these pages you will find the inspiration you need to succeed in every area of your life.

I hope you are excited because life changes now. The fact that you chose this book shows that you are prepared to make improvements and experience the best life has to offer. As your inspirational cheerleader and life coach, I just want to let you know that I believe in you and you are worthy of the success you desire. Further more, whatever changes, alterations and improvements that you need to make you can do it! You have the perfect tool at your finger tips. Just absorb its contents and be inspired and think higher. That's what Success Attraction Notes and Quotes is all about: daily inspiration and quick antidotes to help you change your thinking so you can change your habits so you can live a higher life. You are just an adjustment away from you realizing your dreams, so take this book and use it to shift your thinking, revise your daily routine and begin to live the life you deserve!

Success Note #1

Ask GOD Questions

Take 30 minutes to seek divine guidance today

#1 Ask God Questions

Take the time to ask God questions. We often have to retreat to advance. Benjamin Franklin once said, "The doors of wisdom are never shut." Wisdom is always available to us when we need it; we just need to ask the right questions. When you don't know what's next, ask for it to be revealed to you. Before you rest your conscious mind, ask for inner cues.

Do Q & A before you lay down to rest. Ask about your projects, your opportunities, your next moves and your work. I often ask questions as I go to sleep, only to awaken in the morning with refreshing solutions. When you seek inner cues before you go to bed, you will be more mindful of the outer clues that come your way. Even if you don't pop out of bed with the perfect solution, be patient. Illumination often happens while you are in motion, going about your day.

Illumination often occurs when you are doing something unrelated to the issue at hand. It can happen while showering, driving, listening to music or taking part in another type of activity. So stay alert and keep your ears perked. Eye-opening illumination may be closer than it appears. The key is to be prepared when the answers present themselves.

Purchase a journal for your daily Q& A sessions with God. List your life's questions and fill in the answers as you get them. Ask questions, sit quietly and write down what you hear. Clarification will come once your quandaries are clearly written.

Take Fast Action:

1.Take 30 minutes each day to ask God for direction and insight.

2. This week, take some time and really tune in and get divine direction. Each night before going to bed, write a list of questions that you would like God to answer.

Then, in your morning time of solitude, review the questions, sit quietly and write down all of the answers and ideas that come to you. Often you will awake with an idea or nudge that will lead you to your solution. If not, go on about your day and stay aware and alert. The answers to your questions are sure to unfold.

3. Journalize. Write down your burning questions. What divine solutions do you need right now? Take five minutes and write them now.

SUCCESS ATTRACTION QUOTE NOTES:

I DECREE *ANSWERS*

I DECREE:

I decree that I have every solution I need to be successful in all areas of my life. Money-making ideas and answers come to me daily and I take action quickly and receive outstanding results. I ask God questions and hear the right answers. I am aware of my surroundings and receive inspiration from all that I do and see. I am so grateful that every time I ask God questions, I receive divine direction and clarity for my life and business.

Journal Notes

Journal Notes

Success Note # 2

CHANGE

Takes Precisely As Long As...

YOU THINK IT DOES

Make One Small Change Today and Create a Big Difference

#2 Change Take Precisely as Long as You Think It Does

Change doesn't have to be a long, drawn-out process. Small daily actions can make a big difference. Often when we think of changing our lives, we think of big projects and life-changing shifts, and then get overwhelmed just thinking about self-improvement. In reality, small, daily changes can make a big difference in your life. Dream big and make small changes now. If you're a little overwhelmed by your to-do list or starting to feel paralyzed by the size of your goals, try this:

1. **Write down your goals and read them every day**. Re-writing your top goals every morning will help you focus on what's most important and generate loads of ideas to help you achieve them.

2. **Do one thing you don't want to do each day.** Usually we know exactly where we need to improve our lives, but haven't committed to doing what it takes to change the situation.

3. Take five minutes every morning to visualize your best self. See yourself being a top performer and accomplishing all of your goals. You must see it and believe it before you can achieve it.

Take Fast Action

1. Write a list of the top five areas where you want to see change in your life. Next, take a few minutes to think about the small actions you can take right now to get change under way.

2. Now, make a list of seven small changes you will make over the next seven days.

3. Use your journal pages throughout the week to record your actions and any exciting outcomes.

I DECREE *CHANGE!*

I DECREE:

I decree that I am achieving my goals and dreams at an accelerated rate. I overcome obstacles quickly. Everything in my life is consistently improving everyday. I make the proper changes to live the life I want. I am accomplishing my dreams faster than I ever thought possible and I am very grateful.

Journal Notes

Journal Notes

Success Note # 3

DON'T BE TOO CHEAP TO

List the Books, Audio Programs or Coaching Course You Will Invest in This Month to Improve Your Life

#3 Never Be Too Cheap To Invest In Yourself

Success is a continual process and it requires you to make continual investments in information and resources to increase your income and status. If you're not investing a portion of your income into a financial education, you are stopping and blocking your own ability to make more money. Have you ever noticed that wealthy people have one or more libraries in their home? Wealthy people invest in books, conferences, seminars and other resources to expand their knowledge, ignite creativity and up level their income. If you have a desire for wealth, you must adopt this key principle too.

It is this kind of specific education that saves you time and money so that you can make more money in the end. You can spend one day in a workshop and learn what someone may have take years to develop and perfect. Now more than ever before smart entrepreneurs are fast-tracking their success by learning wealth building secrets that took others years to discover.

I often remind my clients of the value of the information you invest in. If you take a $697 course where you learn and implement a new idea that generates $20,000 for you, then you've had a tremendous return on your investment. At this point you can clearly see how a $697 investment in a course that empowers you to earn $20,000 is a no-brainer right?

Resist the temptation to build your business empire only on free information. Any type of advice that will produce a significant amount of increase for you is worth you investing in. Free advice will keep you at bay on the outskirts of true success. If you desire to build great wealth, it is wise to invest in a great coach to help you get there. Take a course, buy their book or audio program. Build your success library over time. Never be too cheap to invest in yourself, you and your life are certainly worth it!

Take Action Now...

1. Take some time to look over your goals, dreams and desires. Read them out loud and update them as necessary.

2. Answer the following questions: What tools, resources and information do you need to invest in to upgrade your life and build a more profitable business? What mentors, leaders, colleagues or coach do you need to connect with to get from where you are to where you what to be?

3. Today sit down and make a list of all the books, audio programs and coaching courses you will invest in this month to upgrade yourself and improve your life.

SUCCESS ATTRACTION QUOTE NOTES:

I DECREE THAT I *INVEST*

I DECREE:

I decree that I always have more than enough resources to invest in myself, improve and grow. I enjoy being a life-long learner and frequently purchase the books, audio programs, coaching programs and attend live events. My consistent investment in myself expands my thinking, increases my business and upgrades my lifestyle. I am grateful that my commitment to self-improvement attracts unlimited amounts of success into my life daily.

Journal Notes

Journal Notes

Success Note # 3

#4 Create An Environment Conducive To Your Success

Your environment is a key element of your success. We are designed to adapt to our environment. Our attitudes, actions and assessments have a lot to do with the environment we're in. As entrepreneurs, it's important to create an environment that perpetuates success, achievement and results.

Though it may appear to be a small issue, if the surroundings in your home and workspace are not visually pleasant to you, it can hinder your ability to think clearly, be productive or relax. Taking just a few simple steps to improve the appearance of your interiors will help you (as well as your staff or your family) stay motivated to function at the highest levels. The following are three quick ways to add beauty to the space in which you work, live and play. Here are a few things that you can do to upgrade both your work and living spaces to keep you focused on your success.

1. Fix whatever is broken. Does that door jam every time you attempt to open and close it? Does that dysfunctional, leaning office chair need to be laid to rest? What about the kitchen drawer that's off track and never closes properly? Repair the minor interior issues that irritate you every day. You'll be surprised at how much better your day flows when you fix all the little things that frustrate you.

2. Highlight the photographs. Surround yourself with great photos that celebrate your success. Start with pictures that rehearse your victories, then add in more photos that allow you to dream big and declare a wonderful, exciting future. Carefully place reminders, photos, memories and other inspiring images around your office to keep you motivated and comfortable in your workspace. Framed awards, accomplishments, photos with your mentors, celebrities, and monumental moments in life are all great additions to the office.

3. Surround yourself with good books. If you want to get money-making ideas, fill your environment with good books—

and read them. When I'm working on a project, I often just search book titles in my library. Become a collector of great books in your industry as well as books about your hobbies and other interests. Slowly but surely, you'll surround yourself with a tailor-made wealth of knowledge that can almost always spark a new idea, help you finish a good point or develop a new money-making strategy.

Take Fast Action

1. Look around you and make a list of all the small changes you can make right away to upgrade your environment.

2. Evaluate your business and living spaces. Then rearrange one room this week to improve your environment and increase your productivity.

3. Use your journal pages to answer the following questions:

- What does your ideal workspace look like? Describe

it in detail.

• What does your ideal home look like? Describe it in detail.

SUCCESS ATTRACTION QUOTE NOTES:

____

____

____

____

____

____

____

____

____

____

____

____

____

____

____

I DECREE *SUCCESSFUL SURROUNDINGS!*

I DECREE:

I decree that my living and business spaces are conducive for success. I have rearranged my environment and operate at the highest level of productivity each day. I enjoy my beautiful surroundings and I am profitable wherever I work, live and play. I am so grateful that my surroundings are inspiring. I always get the right things done to increase my business and reach my goals.

Journal Notes

Journal Notes

Success Note #5

Make
TODAY
"FIX-IT"
DAY

Write a List of Personal Improvements You Want to Make then Take Action and Fix One Thing Today.

#5 Make Today "Fix It " Day

No matter who you are or what you are striving to become, personal improvement is an essential part of realizing your dreams. However, in my years of coaching, I've come across many people who deeply desire to reach their greatest potential, but lack the insight and instructions to do so. I often say that most dreams die between what to do and how to do them. Here are three keys to get started on your very own personal improvement campaign. They will help you change your thinking and take action to fix whatever is necessary for you to become your absolute best.

1. Get a Vision of What You Want to Become

Keep your eyes on the prize. Make it a habit to envision yourself at your best instead of constantly highlighting your shortcomings. If you constantly focus on your past and all of its mistakes or even try to remain in the glory days of past victories, you'll miss out on all the wonderful things in the future that are headed your way.

2. Become Uncomfortable

You must lose your love for being comfortable if you want to reach your goals. I've always said that the true definition of laziness is the unwillingness to be uncomfortable. To "fix" yourself, you must stretch yourself; work harder; finish faster; face your fears. Trying to stay comfortable lulls us into complacency and is one of the biggest enemies of success. This week, fix up your life by going the extra mile. Stretch yourself and get uncomfortable by taking action. Tell four people you've never met about your business. Work an extra two hours each night on your marketing plans. To get what you've never had, you must do what you've never done. So push yourself to do more during the next seven days.

3. Set New Goals

Set new goals to improve. Take the time to put everything you want to fix in your life in goal form. Goal-setting helps you to define your purpose and stay focused so that you can direct your time and energy properly. Pen your goals. As you write them down you will create a road map for your life.

Take Action Now:

1. Write a list of personal improvements that you want to make; then take action and fix one thing today!

2. For the next 7 days take "uncomfortable action." Do one thing each day towards your goals that makes you uncomfortable.

3. Today write a new list of goals that speak to what you desire to "fix" right now.

SUCCESS ATTRACTION QUOTE NOTES:

I
DECREE
IMPROVEMENT

I DECREE:

I decree that I improve daily. I continually sharpen my skills, make my shortcomings my strengths and strive to be excellent in all that I do. I make the right choices and surround myself with the right people so that I am always moving forward toward greater levels of success.

Journal Notes

Journal Notes

Success Note #6

#6 Frame Your Future with Pictures and Words

To enjoy lifelong success, you must get a picture of what's possible for you and hold fast to that image until it manifests in your life. Next, to get your manifestation process in motion, you must gather images and phrases to illustrate your dreams and inspire you to pursue your goals. Doing this will multiply your power to manifest success many times over. Never underestimate the power of creating visual prompts using real photos and words that you can meditate on often. For example: If your goal is to become a millionaire, write yourself a check for a million dollars.

Successful young entrepreneur Erica Douglas wrote herself a check for $1 million, pasted it on her bathroom mirror and while she brushed her teeth every morning she imagined herself selling her company for a million dollars after taxes. Within one year, she sold her company for $1.1 million, became debt-free and walked away from the deal with $1 million after taxes!

If your goal is to have a New York Times Best Seller, create a mock cover and put The New York Times Best Seller seal on it.

If your goal is to travel to Italy, find a post card of the Leaning Tower of Pisa and paste a picture of yourself in front of it, as if you had taken the picture while you were there on vacation or business.

If your goal is to speak at a large conference, create a speaking itinerary with all the places you want to speak on it. You get the picture, right?

Become relentless about visualizing every day and night and watch how fast you'll begin to manifest your desires!

How to Frame Your Future with Pictures and Words

One of the best visual prompts to use is The Millionaire's Dream Book. It's the perfect tool to help you stay focused on your goals while you are waiting for your dreams to manifest. Your Dream Book acts as your life catalog that helps you to illustrate, describe and explore your dreams in 3D. When used properly, the results are always incredible. The process of filling in your Dream Book causes you to finally awaken your storybook life, because the images you meditate on set up an attraction force that pulls everything toward you.

Take Action Now:

1. If you already have a Dreambook, use the section that helps you to describe your life a year from today! If you don't have your Dreambook yet, write a detailed description in your journal for now.

2. Now based on what you wrote, hunt for and gather the images and words that illustrate what you've written. Pull out articles, pictures from magazines, captions or ads that jump out at you.

3. Next cut-out the pictures and put them on your goal cards, storyboard or in your Millionaire Dream Book.

4. Finally, post your images and words where you will see it often.

SUCCESS ATTRACTION QUOTE NOTES:

I DECREE *A BRIGHT FUTURE*

I DECREE:

I decree that I can
see my Future
I decree that I frame my
future for success. I am diligent
in my pursuit of my dreams and
goals. I faithfully
use daily triggers such as my
vision boards, goals cards and
success strategies to keep my
nspiration in plain sight and
stay focused on my success. I
am so grateful that I
accomplish my goals faster than
I imagined because I frame my
future with pictures and words.

Journal Notes

Journal Notes

Success Note #7

Make TODAY "FIX-IT" DAY

Write a List of Personal Improvements You Want to Make then Take Action and Fix One Thing Today.

#7 Today is a Great Day So Expect the Best

Want to have the best day ever—day after day? Maintain a positive attitude.

Positivity is what you need in your life right now to accomplish great things. Just as negative talk can stop your flow of increase...positive talk can ramp it up into high gear! Many times, you can be right on the brink of bigness and being set up for a money shift! With a positive outlook and attitude you can literally walk right into your biggest breakthrough yet! Decide first thing that "Today is going to be a great day!" Choose to be happy and let your joy shine through. The better you feel, the better life becomes. Radiate positivity today and watch things happen!

Infusing your mind with positive thoughts and shaping your world with positive words will cause you to produce more positive results in your life. Right now you're getting as many opportunities as you think you can have. You're making just the amount of money you really believe you can. To break into making what you've only dreamed of and wished for, you must start thinking, believing and speaking like you're already worth that number!

A positive mind gives a profitable outcome. So fight to think positive and express a positive mood. If you're ready to make more increase in your business, seal more deals, attract new clients...then you have to SHIFT your thinking. Here are a few keys to help you stick to your plan to stay positive:

1. Listen to positive music and audio programs.

2. Surround yourself with positive people.

3. Keep your conversation happy and uplifting.

Positive energy is contagious that's why it's so important to think and expect the best. What ever you are thinking or feeling, you're projecting to others around you. When you enter a room and you are thinking negatively, you project that negativ-

ity to everyone in the room. Likewise, when you think positive, you project positivity to everyone else too.
Another way to stay positive is to adopt an attitude of gratitude. What you are thankful and grateful for will multiply in your life. Start your day thinking about what is good in your life, what is going right. It's nearly impossible to have a down day when you have a thankful heart.

So what's the big pay off for all of this positive effort? Seeing your life improve in every way in direct proportion to your positive words and new successful thinking.

Take Fast Action

1.Take five minutes to imagine and expect the best! See yourself having a great day. Imagine yourself producing and earning more.

2. Say this ten times today: "If anything can go good it will. I focus only on the good and expect only the best!"

3. Write a gratitude list. Grab your journal and write down everything you are grateful for. Take time to be thankful for your blessings and achievements.

SUCCESS ATTRACTION QUOTE NOTES:

I DECREE *A GREAT DAY*

I DECREE:

I decree that today is
a great day! I only expect
the best and great things
happened for me everyday. I
am grateful for my
blessings and believe
only the best things
in life are coming my way.

Journal Notes

Journal Notes

Success Note # 8

IMAGE is Everything!

Create A Plan Today to Upgrade Your Look and Prepare for Your Next Level of Success

#8 Image is Everything

Your personal and brand image are a huge key to your success. Especially for the entrepreneur, a big part of advancing in life is looking the part.

Fair or not, studies show that we humans are visual creatures. We initially trust, buy and connect based on what we see. Whether you are pursuing a promotion, seeking more clients or simply striving to build a better life, a keen sense of style when it comes to your image can lead to greater opportunities and higher levels of success. Here are a few quick tips to polish your personal and brand image to set yourself up for success.

1. Nail it.

Nail your first impression every time by keeping your hands well-manicured and pampering your feet with frequent pedis. To wardrobe my nails, my favorite is Superstar Nail Lacquer's fast-drying formula and chic colors. It helps me be fabulous down to the detail without taking forever.

2. Become a student of style.

Get a working knowledge of all things fashionable, so you can develop your "what to wear wisdom" and then allow your personal style to shine through. Stay updated with trend reports, street style and fashion spotlight offerings to keep you at the top of your game when it comes to getting gorgeous.

3. Dress the part.

Start dressing for the role you want. It's just "acting as if" with a fashionable twist. Review your goals: Where can you "act as if" and then dress the part? For example, you could act as if you're the CEO of your own super successful company, where you make the kind of money you want, drive what you want, etc. Now, what does this very successful you look like? Get a vivid picture in your mind. Next, think of what you can do to style yourself as closely as possible to the image you just imagined. This is not about being phony, but rather preparing yourself for an opportunity that doesn't exist yet. As you role-play your dreams via your dress code, you'll set yourself up to star in your own real-life success story.

4. Upgrade your look with the right hairstyle. Experts say one of the best ways to instantly upgrade your image is to improve your hairstyle. So put your bad hair days behind you and head to the best salon in your area or collaborate with your present hairdresser. Get a hairstyle that affords you the ability to look fabulous daily.

5. Become the spokesperson for your brand. When it comes to your business, remember that no matter what industry you are in, you are the number one representative for your brand. Your personal appearance has a great effect on your brand and income opportunities. As the spokesperson for your business and life, it's your job to always look your best in person and online. Doing this will help you remove any image barriers to achieving your dreams and goals. Create a plan today to upgrade your look and prepare for your next level of success.

Take Fast Action

1. Schedule an appointment this week to upgrade some aspect of your image. Do you need to upgrade your hairstyle? Do you nails need a bit of TLC? Make time for a bit of self-care this week.

2. Within the next 7 days go to the bookstore and grab a few of the top fashion magazines. Flip through the pages and pull out the outfits and images that speak to you. Make a vision board of your new successful image.

3. Use your journal pages in this section to write about what you want to achieve this year and how you can start dressing for the role you want right now.

I DECREE AN *IMAGE* UPGRADE

I DECREE:

I decree that I am always dressed for success. I carry myself with dignity and honor. My outer appearance is always a reflection of my successful mentality. I am so grateful that I always have enough to fund my beauty and fashion regimens. I am consistently promoted and have favor because I always look the part.

Journal Notes

Journal Notes

Success Note #9

You Don't Have a *Increase* Problem You Have an *Idea* Problem

Today Sit Quietly and Write Down 40 Ways You Can INCREASE Your INCOME in the Next 30 Days

#9 You Don't Have an Increase Problem You Have an Idea Problem

Great ideas are the beginning to all fortunes. Fresh, new, innovative thoughts lead to the creative solutions that can drastically increase your income. That's why it's important to stay inspired and keep your creativity flowing. Following the same routine at home day after day can become mundane after awhile. It's important to shake things up a bit to stay sharp and full of fresh ideas. Here's a list of 10 ways you can charge your creative juices. Take action on at least one of them this week. You just may come up with your next million-dollar idea!

10 Ways to Stay Creative and Generate Great Ideas

1. Find your think spot.

Find a clean, quiet spot where you can sit and think. There

will be times when your mind calls for stimulation to get your creative juices flowing. Yet, more often than not, creativity needs a quiet place to cultivate.

2. Write freely.

Write uninhibited thoughts early in the morning when you first wake up to jump-start your creativity. Brilliant ideas, solutions and reminders will come early in the morning.

3. Keep an idea journal with you at all times.

Whether you love a pen and a pad or you use a notepad app, when inspiration strikes, record it quickly right when the idea is fresh.

4. Use sticky notes.

Record a single thought; then later you can rearrange your ideas into a flow that fits your project.

5. Meditate.

Clear your mind through meditation. Get in tune with your

inner spirit and allow yourself to hear divine ideas that are meant for you.

6. Break your routine.

We are all creatures of habit and doing the same things over and over can dull your mind. Break up the monotony and do things a little different.

7. Get moving.

Ride a bike, run on the treadmill, exercise and get your blood pumping. The increased blood flow positively impacts your creative juices.

8. Take a walk.

Fresh air and natural surroundings will inspire you.

9. Get sunshine.

Sunshine improves your mood, which is also good for your creativity.

10. Add color for creativity.

Colors have been known to enhance your mood and impact your thinking. Go for the color green when you want to be more creative and the color yellow when you want to enhance your mood overall (which also helps your creativity).

Take Fast Action

1. Get out your journal and write down your creative idea action plan. Schedule when you will implement each one of these ideas over the next seven days.

2. Today, sit quietly and write down 40 ways you can increase your income in the next 30 days.

3. Schedule a "Fun Day." Plan a day dedicated to having fun and enjoying life. Creativity often strikes in the midst of happy thoughts and good times. I've had many great ideas come to me while having a wonderful time with my friends and family.

I
DECREE
IDEAS FOR INCREASE

I DECREE:

I decree that my great ideas always increase my income. Daily, I make the most of my time of solitude and meditate on my success. I am so grateful that great ideas, solutions, strategies and plans come to me easily and effortlessly. I take fast action on my increase ideas and always enjoy profitable results.

Journal Notes

Journal Notes

Success Note #10

Stay FOCUSED with *Every Day* TRIGGERS

Review Your Goals and Evaluate Your Environment Place your Goal Cards, Storyboards and Other Success Props in Plain View.

Stay Focused with Everyday Triggers

Over the years, I have found that creating daily success triggers are a great tool to keep you focused and on task during your success attraction process. Daily triggers help to speed up the success attraction process by giving you a consistent reminder of what you should be thinking about and working toward. What is a daily success trigger? It is a visual and physical reminder of your goals and intentions. Storyboards, photos, and your favorite quotes are all daily triggers. You must constantly feed your mind with successful images. As you surround yourself with daily success triggers, you will spark new ideas that will lead to new opportunities that open up to you and bring you closer to accomplishing your goals. Here are a few of my favorite daily triggers that have helped me time and time again as I worked through the success attraction process.

Goal Cards

One success trigger that I rely on heavily to stay focused in my business and life is my Goal Cards. The simple action of placing my goals on Goal Cards allows me to focus on one goal at a time and track my success over time. My Goal Cards are the perfect size. They have a space for a photo and a place to write your goal and an achievement date. They are small enough that you can tape them to your computer, your bathroom mirror, refrigerator or anywhere you can frequently see them. They remind you of your goal and by seeing it often and meditating on it, you attract it into your life at a much faster rate.

Stacia's Success Stickies

During the years I have come to love using sticky notes for success triggers so much that I eventually created my own line, Success Stickies. They are just the right size to hold one complete power thought that you may want to be reminded of daily. Often, I use stickies to remind me of my weekly income goals for the company. I can write the number on a sticky and put it on my laptop where I can see it often. Then as I work, I remind myself of the weekly goal and use it as motivation to reach it.

You can also use them as Success Scripts:

Write positive statements on sticky notes and put them in places where you will run across them throughout your day. When you see them, say what's written out loud.

Here are some examples:

On your refrigerator: *"I always make the right food choices and keep up healthy eating habits."*

As a bookmark: *"I have superior knowledge to learn and apply this information."*

On your desk at work: *"Clients come to me daily!"*

In your wallet: *"I have more than enough and my accounts are always full."*

Storyboards

When you storyboard, you create a visual plan that lays out your dreams, goals and desires in sequence. These pictures, coupled with your imagination and faith, create a powerful momentum in your life to draw you closer to your dreams. I storyboard every area of my life. I have used the concept of storyboarding to upgrade my wardrobe, develop a great network, plan my conferences, product lines, television shows and many other things.

Everyone should have a visual board of what they are trying to accomplish for the year! Include pictures, words, crowd shots, uniforms, goals and more. For a more creative or even corporate feel, post your storyboard up on a corkboard. You can use fabric swatches, textiles, photos, sketches, notes, cards, poems, quotes and any other written information that sparks you. Your board is a constant inspiration for ideas and improvement.

Sip and Say Cup

This is a success trigger that my entire staff uses. My Sip and Say cup helps our staff stay focused on our daily money goals. We fill our cups and declare "Making money is easy!" again and again throughout the day. That added focus and quick affirmation spoken repeatedly has made a big difference in our sales.

Take Fast Action

1.Create your storyboard this week. Next, post it up where you can review it often. Take time to stop and meditate on it each morning before you start your day.

2. Review your goals and evaluate your environment. Next, place your Goal Cards, storyboards and other success props in plain view.

3. Write down short, powerful affirmations on your Success Stickies and post them up where they cannot be missed. Every time you're reminded, say your positive statement out loud.

SUCCESS ATTRACTION QUOTE NOTES:

I DECREE FOCUS

I DECREE:

I decree that I stay focused on my success. I faithfully use my everyday triggers such as my Goal Cards and Success Stickies to keep my aspirations in plain sight. I am focused on my dreams and goals, therefore divine solutions, connections and opportunities are attracted to me every day.
My daily triggers keep me on track and I always achieve my goals.

Journal Notes

Journal Notes

Success Note #11

INFORMATION CHANGES the Seasons of our Lives!

Today Hunt for and Gather Books, Magazines and Programs to Flood Your Mind with New Insight

#11 Information Changes the Seasons of Our Lives

Want to improve the overall quality of your life? Would you like to experience continued success no matter what your age or season in life? Then engage in the lifelong practice to hunt and gather new information. Winners, leaders and all who succeed, read. Stay on a constant quest for quality information and then continue even further with mind-expanding experiences. Make the bookstore your favorite hot spot. Study, see and do the best you can on every level of life. As you do, you will raise your lifestyle and set yourself up for a fabulous future.

What kind of information do you love to hunt for and gather? It may be a clue to your future.

☐ What area of the bookstore do you gravitate to?

☐ What books are on your shelf right now?

☐ What magazines do you love to read?

☐ What stirs you up? What gets you fully energized? What gives you tons of energy when you do it?

Become passionate about hunting for and gathering new information. It is easier for your mind to produce new ideas and answers when flooded with fresh knowledge. I'm living proof: Gathering the right information changed my life. Years ago, I was frustrated and trying to figure out how to do everything to succeed as an author, speaker and businesswoman. No one told me what to do. I studied for hours, read book after book, went through program after program ... then, I finally got the fight in me to not let anything stop me from pursuing my passion and learning how to profit from doing what I loved to do.

I went to conference after conference, hunting and gathering, networking with gurus and interviewing the best. I overcame my struggle to succeed by investing in any information I could get my hands on, from the top people in my industry. I started where I could and eventually bought tons of materials and programs, then went through them all to figure out what to do until it clicked. I listed all of the information I desperately needed. I remember making a chart of products and programs to get from my mentors and I crossed items off that list one by one until I had them all—and I do mean all of them.

As I began putting the information that I was learning into practice and started taking fast action, I had a sudden shift and I shocked myself when I tripled my income within 30 days! After I began to duplicate my success, it hit me: Information had truly changed the season of my life.

And that was the beginning of how I learned how to turn my passion into profit and began to teach others how to do the same. Now, I have it all down to a science; a proven formula that works again and again. My systems and methods are solid and my coaching clients love getting such profitable results. Today, take time to hunt for and gather books, magazines and programs to flood your mind with new insight.

Take Fast Action

1. Take a trip to the bookstore and make note of all the books and magazines that stand out to you. What subjects and topics do you love the most? Make note of them.

2. Grab your journal and list all of the ways in which you want to improve. In what areas would you like to become more profitable? Where can you get the information you need to take your life to the next level? Write it down and make a plan to acquire it.

3. Take one evening this week to begin to absorb some of the information you've gathered. Read, study and listen to an audio program. Start soaking up the new information so you can begin to fast-forward your life into a new season.

I DECREE A NEW SEASON

I DECREE:

I decree that each day I absorb information that leads to my success. I frequently hunt for and gather books, magazines and programs that flood my mind with new insight. I habitually improve my knowledge, wisdom and mentality, which results in a lifetime of success.

Journal Notes

Journal Notes

Success Note #12

#12 Cultivate Possibility Thinking

You must learn to dream big—really big! Start believing that great things are possible for you. You deserve to have everything in your life exactly the way you want it! Think BIG—don't let the mindset of others limit you!

Let's begin with defining what you really want—your ideal life in all areas of your life and business. Picture your business in its best possible state. Picture a loving, successful family and an enjoyable personal life. Now take that dream you just thought about and take it up 10 levels. Now you're dreaming!

Why is dreaming big the first step? Because your life can rise no higher than your thoughts will permit it. I agree with a quote by Oliver Wendell Holmes, who said (paraphrased), "A mind once stretched by a new idea can never return to its original size." So I am going to ask you to cultivate possibility thinking and dream really BIG.

Cultivating possibility thinking is about upgrading your mentality and your life—no downgrading allowed! I've watched so many people go through life saying, "I don't want much," playing a role they call humble, yet they are just miserable! They aren't reaching their goals; they're living an average existence, stuck in a rut and losing hope daily.

Now, it's your time to cultivate your mind and THINK BIG. I want you to take this very seriously. You may have heard of positive thinking before and may have even tried it for a few days—but this time is different. I want you to think big as if your entire life depends on it ... because it does! Thinking big will cause you to course-correct your destiny and create a long-lasting legacy for your children and their children. When you think big, you achieve big and when you achieve big, you get to make a real difference in the world.

Take Fast Action

1. Without pondering for a long time, write out a list of possibilities. List some of the ways things can happen.

2. Take 15 minutes to dream beyond your means. Imagine the possibilities in detail. See in your mind's eye the how, when and where of your dreams coming to pass.

3. Schedule a time within the next seven days where you will take action on at least one thing on your list of possibilities.

SUCCESS ATTRACTION QUOTE NOTES:

I DECREE *BIG DREAMS*

I DECREE:

I decree that I consistently cultivate possibility thinking. Daily, I take time to dream beyond my means and imagine good things happening in my business and life. I will increase my ability to do these things by engaging in mind-expanding experiences. As I see, hear and do more, I cultivate my belief in what's possible for me. I believe my dreams are attainable.

Journal Notes

Journal Notes

Success Note #12

Surround *Yourself* with "GET IT" people.

Today evaluate your 5 closest relationships. Draw closer to those who celebrate your success. Distance Yourself from those who don't.

#13 Surround Yourself with "Get It People"

One of the biggest components to living a successful life is being connected to the right people. You will often hear me talk on the importance of relationships, because there is no getting around the fact that you will become like those you surround yourself with.

Build a network of "get it" people. These are people who understand who you are, where you're going and what life should be like. Who are you allowing to accompany you on your life's journey? Are they cheerleaders or critics? Assess their lives. Do you want to become like them? Do you want the results that they are experiencing? If you answered no to either of these questions, then it's time to re-evaluate and upgrade your inner circle. There is so much to gain by filling your inner circle with people who simply "get it." They get your goals, dreams and celebrate you every step of the way. Success is a collection of right relationships! For example, I have set up my coaching forums for my clients to connect, network and build a community that is beneficial to all. If you want to set yourself up for lifelong success, you will need to become very discerning about your relationships.

Are you in relationships with those who consistently add value to your life?
How you are living your purpose today is a result of:

- Who you've decided to spend time with ...
- Who you've decided to learn from ...
- Who you've decided to believe ...
- Who you've decided to look like ...

Learn to associate higher than where you are right now. Of course, it's not an easy task—high achievers are often busy and very hard to connect with. However, don't let the obstacles stop you from connecting. Associating higher is not always comfortable, but it is certainly always profitable.

Observe the five closest people in your inner circle. Take inventory of their lifestyles, income and relationships. You are the sum total of who you are around. If you ask, the right people will come into your life:

- To give you a fresh perspective …
- To help you find your potential …
- To create or provide a platform for you …
- To add fans to your purpose …
- To show you how to frame your life for prosperity …

Also, I want to encourage you to associate with a coach. Having somebody believe in you and push you in the right direction, with the right information, is key to successful living. If you truly want to enrich your life, you must be willing to follow the faith and formula of someone who has already achieved high levels of success. Whenever you're ready to go higher, you will always need a teacher. A successful coach will have your clues and give you a clear picture of what is possible.So start today! Get an inner circle of get it people to hang around.

☐ Search for the people who get your purpose, your position and your projects. Conversations with get it people can ignite new dreams for you.

☐ Pay the price to get in the presence of the people who understand who you are and where you are headed. Go to conferences, workshops and gatherings where they hang out!

Take Fast Action

Here is a quick, easy way to evaluate your relationships.

1. Write down the names of your five closest friends.

2. Ask the following questions in regards to each friend:

a. What do they have me doing?
b. What do they have me talking about?
c. Where do they have me going?
d. How do they add value to my life?

e. Should I maintain this relationship?

3. After your evaluation, note which relationships you will spend more time nurturing and which ones you will ease away from.

SUCCESS ATTRACTION QUOTE NOTES:

I DECREE *NEW RELATIONSHIPS*

I DECREE:

I decree that I'm only surrounded by those who celebrate my success. I am wise in my relationships. I connect higher, with the right mentors and coaches, and stay on the fast track to success. I connect with my purpose partners and have a powerful network that promotes me and empowers me to promote others. I have favor with influential people in high places and I properly nurture my relationships with people who want the best for me.

Journal Notes

Journal Notes

Success Note #14

People Do What You INSPECT not What You EXPECT

Today Examine Your Business and Household. Then Create a Plan to Inspire Your Team and Family to Achieve More

#14 People Do What You Inspect Not What You Expect

To successfully run your business and your household, you will eventually have to master the art of delegation. Overseeing a big vision requires that you enlist others to get big things done. One of the most important truths to remember when delegating in any situation is that people do what you inspect, not what you expect. This simply means that if you want a successful outcome when delegating a task or project to someone, you must clearly communicate what you want done, how you want it done and check throughout the process to make sure it's being done correctly.

Don't just expect for things to come out right in the end; inspect the work along the way so that you will be pleased with the outcome.

The temptation here is to say, "Forget it, I will just do it myself." Truthfully, (especially as an entrepreneur), there may be many tasks that you could easily perform yourself that are more challenging for your staff to complete. However, attempting to do everything yourself can lead to you being overburdened with routine work and lacking sufficient time to spend on higher-level tasks that only you can do.

Studies show that 80 percent of a leader's time is spent on operational details, such as gathering information and organizing meetings, while only 20 percent of their work week is spent on the kind of high-level thinking that will grow their business, improve their household and increase their income. Therefore, learning the art of delegation really is important to your success. Here are a few handy tips to follow when delegating tasks to your team.

1. Determine what should be delegated and what would be better for you to do. Ask yourself the following questions:

☐ Am I devoting enough time to focusing on key goals and long-term project planning?

☐ Is my desk overflowing with uncompleted tasks?

☐ Am I getting buried in paper and routine?

☐ What am I doing that someone else could be doing?

☐ What am I doing that only I can or should do?

2. Determine to whom you will delegate the task. Check an individual's track record. Have they proven themselves to be reliable in the past?

3. Provide clear instructions and guidelines.

4. Establish deadlines. Determine when tasks need to be completed or when a final project is due. If you are delegating a long or extensive project, set scheduled checkpoints to evaluate progress and discuss any difficulties.

5. Allow your delegates an opportunity to ask questions and clarify instructions.

6. Schedule feedback sessions to see how the project is going, what new ideas have surfaced and what they have accomplished so far. Don't deny a delegate the chance to learn by interfering too much.

7. Always be positive when reviewing and expect to hear good news.

8. Provide direction and suggest resources to your delegates on challenging projects, but don't do all of the legwork. Remember delegation is supposed to save you time and stretch the delegate.

9. Give the process time. Release more responsibility slowly and gradually over time, as your delegates produce excellent, quality work.

10. Reward any extra effort when you see it. Send an email and/or tell your delegate that they did a great job on the project.

Take Fast Action

1. Today, examine your business and household. Then create a plan to inspire your team and family to achieve more.

2. Write a list of tasks you need to delegate.

3. Within the next two weeks, enlist some help. Hire an assistant, recruit an intern, go online and get a virtual assistant—find which option fits your life best and delegate your routine tasks so you can focus on what's important.

SUCCESS ATTRACTION QUOTE NOTES:

I DECREE *SUCCESSFUL DELEGATION*

I DECREE:

I decree that I am an inspiration to those around me. I properly plan for the success of **my business and household, then inspire both my business team and my** family to do their best. I am diligent and have the proper systems in place to follow up with the instructions that are given. I am so grateful that as a whole, all of our efforts lead to success.

Journal Notes

Journal Notes

Success Note #15

#15 Become A Life Long Learner

If I told you that I knew a secret process that I guaranteed would help you make more money, look great, get promoted, change careers, upgrade your social status, and be personally fulfilled, would you try it? Would you enjoy your life after making all of those improvements? Though this miracle process is not actually a secret, it is not as widely used as it should be. The process is called learning, and it can improve your life immensely. Life becomes so much more satisfying when there is a constant flow of learning.

The art of learning is about making the most of the opportunities made available to you, which empowers you to live a life that is more exciting and wonderful than you ever imagined. Developing, enriching and reinventing one's life has become the mantra of our society today. What you don't know can greatly hinder your success in life. You must get informed.

People experience lack, miss opportunities and even lose their lives, just because they don't have the proper information. Anyone who expects to keep up with the pace of a technologically advanced, well-traveled, highly connected, excessively informed world, must expose themselves to lifelong learning.

Studying the right information is necessary for financial increase, job advancement, and even relating to our children (they learn so fast these days). This does not mean that you must go to the closest university and sign over your life for enrollment. What it does mean is that you should always be a student in life. Learning must be weaved into your daily practice.

Here are a few helpful hints on how to study and keep your mind and your spirit prepared to achieve.

Take Fast Action

Study strategies

1. Evaluate your life, your business and your passions and determine what topics are important to you.

Write them all down.

2. Now narrow down your list to the top five subjects that you need to stay educated on to continue becoming successful at what you do. Now that you have the right topics to focus on, let's create your study habits that will lead to top performance.

3. Create a study habit by choosing a certain time and/or day that you study.

4. Collect what you need. Make sure you have all of your information and materials on hand.

5. Create a study pattern. Determine the process you will use for studying. For example, you could:

- Meditate quietly for a few minutes to think about what you need to learn
- Read your information
- Record notes

- Review your notes
- Ponder the information

6. Fight tiredness and boredom by taking a nap, eating light beforehand, turning down the heat, drinking cold water and eliminating sweet snacks.

7. Keep all of your study tools in one place (i.e., a basket on your desk, by your bedside, in a briefcase, etc.).

8. Write down the subject you are studying, and any relevant information you come across, in your study journal.

I DECREE *MY LOVE FOR LEARNING*

I DECREE:

I decree that I am a lifelong learner. I enjoy absorbing information that inspires and empowers me to be a top performer. I am an avid reader. My commitment to learning makes me more money, creates better opportunities and continually upgrades my entire life. I easily and effortlessly grasp all of the concepts, principles, strategies and information that lead to my continued success.

Journal Notes

Journal Notes

Success Note #16

#16 Live By Lists

Are you ready to opt out of stressful living and enjoy overwhelming success? Learn to list your life. ... Yes, it's that simple!

It is a fact that unless there is a system in your mind, your mind will not let go of what needs to be done. Consequently, your brain will keep churning and you'll feel constant pressure until you develop a system to handle your life's running to-do list.

Writing a list provides you with a system, which helps you to remove pressure and improve your performance in work and in life. Listing your life daily will bring about solutions and help you keep an orderly state of mind, so that creativity can abound. I LIVE BY LISTS! This practice is one of my greatest success tools. When you list your life, you lock yourself into a success system that works time and time again. I am convinced that my pen and paper empower me to progress and can do the same for you. Lists:

☐ Prevent you from forgetting life's important things

☐ Stimulate more progress by helping you to keep a clear vision

☐ Create an easy way to organize yourself and get more of the right things done

☐ Help you be more effective in coordinating daily activities

You cannot lead effectively without a habit of listing. It's a simple yet powerful solution for success that you can practice daily.

Take Fast Action

Twelve lists you should write to live a successful life:

1. List your life's goals.
2. List your daily to-dos.
3. List all the places you want to visit and why.
4. List 30 things you appreciate about your mate.
5. List 12 things you are thankful for. Grateful people do great things.
6. List what you need to purchase. Have a list every time you shop and you will save money.
7. List everything that you need to clean.
8. List all the things you should give away or sell.
9. List what you will do to upgrade your spiritual life.
10. List 20 things that you love about yourself.
11. List 25 things you can do to make more money (write this list daily).
12. List your victories: Where have you done well? Write down your successes.

Please note: Don't assume your list will create superpowers; there are still only 24 hours in a day. But, lists will create the focus to help you be more productive and finish faster.

I DECREE
I LIVE BY LISTS

I DECREE:

I decree that I experience, accomplish and acquire all of the dreams and goals that I have listed. I live by my lists and live an orderly, abundant and fulfilling life. My daily to-do and other lists help me stay focused and attract success in every area of my life. Due to my lists, I am more productive and much more profitable.

Journal Notes

Journal Notes

Success Note #17

MAKING MONEY IS EASY!

This Week Focus On Easily Attracting 5 New Customers, Clients or Contracts

#17 Making Money Is Easy

Making money really is easy! We have developed a "making money is easy" mentality throughout our offices and it has made a tremendous difference in every aspect of our company. Our profits rose significantly higher when we adopted this philosophy into our office culture, and we are happily helping hundreds of entrepreneurs produce the same results. Here is a look at our formula to help you adopt a "making money is easy" philosophy of life and produce your own profitable results.

People become wealthy every day. In fact, millionaires are made every five minutes in this country—so why can't it be you? Millionaires come in all shapes, sizes and colors; from all cultures and ethnic backgrounds—why can't it be you? Eighty percent of millionaires are first-generation millionaires and did not inherit their wealth. More than 7 million households in the U.S. are at millionaire status. Why can't it be you?

I'm here to tell you that it can be you! It all starts with your belief. For this section to be most effective, you must allow yourself to believe that "Making money is easy!" Wealth and abundance are attainable for you, but you need permission from your core beliefs. These beliefs, along with your choices, have brought you where you are today. It is essential to assess your current way of thinking to ensure you stay on track and accomplish your goals. You must be a millionaire in your mind before you ever see the funds in your bank account. Throughout my years of coaching and helping others make millions, I have noticed that there are specific behaviors and ways of thinking that lead to good success.

Adopt the following principles to get your mind trained for a "making money is easy" way of life...

1. Believe. When striving for success, there is no room for doubt. While pursuing exciting goals like attaining wealth, you must lock your mind on the positive and trust that as you take the proper action, your dreams will be realized. To make it past obstacles and setbacks, you have to adopt a winning philosophy. Think, "If anything can go well, it will for me!" Believe that the world is conspiring to help you succeed every day.

2. Be willing to invest in your success. There's a price to pay to learn what you need to know in order to succeed. Most dreams die between what to do and how to do it. Take the limits off and deem yourself valuable enough to make an investment for your future. When you are going for your goals and make the right investments, you often yield a higher return than you even thought possible. One of my clients left her job of 20 years to start a preschool. She invested in coaching to learn how to get her business up and running. Within the first few months she made 13 times the amount she paid for coaching.

3. Be willing to share your greatness with the world. What are people often coming to you for advice about? What would you do for free? This is your unique offering to the world. Now package it and monetize it so that you and the world benefit. Walt Disney was determined to share his greatness with the world no matter what obstacles he faced. At just twenty-one years of age, he and his brother Roy scraped together sufficient funds to build a studio and a team of hotshot animators. He then created a successful series called Oswald and the Lucky Rabbit. But his distributors poached the entire staff and worse, duped him out of the Oswald character. But Disney didn't let that destroy him. He just got on with dreaming big, believing in miracles and allowing magic to happen. And that's when he created a certain talking mouse.

And the rest as they say is history. And what a history! Disney was the first to use synchronized sound in cartoons, the first to use color, the first to make an animated feature and the first to build a theme park. Not only did he monetize his greatness in an incredible way, millions around the world have benefited from Walt Disney's vision that he was determined to share.

4. Take a no-excuse approach. Never make excuses; take action. Excuses are a great way to get friendly with failure. Don't let that be you. Life happens to us all. When you're going for your goals, you have to fight through moments of insecurity, the fear of the unknown and all other obstacles that may arise. Decide you are going to win and keep pressing forward. Highly successful people keep it moving without excuse. They step up to the plate, take responsibility and bring change. Average people hide behind their circumstances, place blame and remain the same. With the proper thinking, a plan to package your expertise and a positive "I-will-win-no-matter-what" attitude, making money really is easy.

Take Fast Action

Connect and commit to the philosophy that making money is easy. Here are some action steps to get you started.

1. Add to your daily affirmations "Making money is easy for me." and say it daily.

2. Write down three ways that you can "monetize your greatness." What do you know or what can you do that others would be willing to pay for?

3. Take action on the things that you have written down within the next 7 days.

4. Learn something new. Invest in a book, program or seminar that will upgrade your skills and increase your value to the world.

I DECREE *MAKING MONEY IS EASY*

I DECREE:

I decree that making money is easy for me. I always generate much more money than I spend. Everything and every one around me prospers me. Daily I meditate on the right things and easily attract new customers, contracts and more cash flow every week. I am so grateful that money comes to me every day and in every way.

Journal Notes

Journal Notes

Success Note #18

#18 Master the Art of Solitude

Quiet time is for seeing, saying and praying. No success can be achieved or sustained without quality "think time." To make attracting success a daily habit instead of a one-time event, you must add times of solitude into your daily routine. By creating a daily routine that includes times of solitude, you can easily create a habit of attracting success in all areas of your life. For many years I have made it a practice to enjoy times of solitude daily. It is one of the key elements to my success.

Every morning I get up about one hour earlier than my family to frame my future and focus my mind-set to prepare for a successful, productive, inspiring day. I lay in bed completely relaxed; the temperature is perfect, and just enough sunshine peeks through my back windows. I stay snuggled under my comforter, with my eyes closed.

I don't fall back to sleep during this time, instead I DREAM BIG. I use this power hour to think about ideas. I write an email or sales page in my head. I craft all the ways I can profit; sometimes I develop a new product. I think about projects I'm working on. I visualize myself being successful and productive with my day.

I visualize my goals being accomplished and me winning in LIFE! I see myself living exactly how I want to live. I even visualize myself in the image and package of success. My body is in great shape; my health in top condition. I use this time to succeed in my mind, and over the years many of those ideas and plans have crystallized and manifested. This powerful practice will keep you focused on success.

Your mind will work to achieve whatever you are focused on. It will cause you to become aware of anything that will help you achieve the goals you have set and constantly visualize and affirm. It activates your subconscious mind to create solutions for achieving the goals you want. So it's important in your time of solitude to focus on solutions and embrace the possibilities.

As you do this, you'll start waking up in the morning with new ideas; you'll find yourself having ideas in the shower, when you're taking walks and while you are driving to work. Never underestimate the power of having time alone to ponder, plan and dream. Solitude is one of life's most valuable treasures; it gives us a "feel better" freedom from the demands of others and times to delight in our time alone.

Take Fast Action

Tomorrow morning, set your alarm 15 minutes earlier. Then, begin your day first in quiet meditation and solitude. Visualize everything you will accomplish that day. Visualize the best possible outcome to every situation. Visualize yourself reaching your goals and feeling happy, productive and successful. Continue this practice regularly.

I DECREE *SUCCESS IN MY SOLITUDE*

I DECREE:

I decree that my quiet time is profitable. I have mastered the art of solitude. My daily routine of pondering and putting my thoughts on paper always pays off. As I sit quietly, I hear the answers I need to succeed in all that I do.

Journal Notes

Journal Notes

Success Note #19

EVERY THING YOU WANT

Is on the Other Side of What You Wont Do.

Today Do One Thing You've Never Done to Get What You've Never Had

#19 Everything You Want is on the Other Side of What You Won't Do

Great success takes great effort. I am a firm believer that you can live your dreams and accomplish great things in life. However, the key is that your passion to succeed must match your effort. High achievers are willing to do what others won't do. They continue on when others are ready to quit.

Often when coaching my business clients, I pose the question, "How bad do you want it?" In other words, are you willing to do what you haven't done to get what you've never had? Extraordinary lives take extraordinary effort. So as you strive for greater levels of success and fulfillment, here are a few effective tips and trains of thought that will help you "get to the other side" by taking the right actions to see your dreams manifest.

Tip #1: Create a new work ethic, then put in the work

Remember, your current work ethic has brought you this far. So in order to achieve, become and have more, you must do more. Your dream life and great success do not come packaged with an excessive amount of rest. I only allow myself to rest or play when I have completed my goals for the day. Every 24 hours is precious, so I make the most of it. A great work ethic does wonders for getting dreams done. Yes, I make time to nurture my relationships with my husband and children, as well as make time to take care of myself. I enjoy my life. We work hard and play hard. I just make it a point to never spend more time relaxing than I do reaching for my goals.

The key is to make sure you are being productive and not just busy. There's a huge difference. Productive means that you're actually completing tasks, making progress and getting the right things done daily. Consider this: What can you do for 30 minutes a day that would put you ahead of the game? Again, nearly everything you want is on the other side of what you've been too lazy (or comfortable) to do. Evaluate each day. Where can you add new systems, avoid distractions and make the most of your time in order to get more things done?

Tip #2: Be excellent

It takes a bit of extra effort to operate in excellence, but it's important that you strive to be excellent in all that you do. According to Webster's Dictionary, to be excellent means possessing outstanding quality or superior merit; remarkably good. Excellence isn't about being gifted or incredibly talented, it's more about being incredibly dedicated to doing even the little things right. In a Harvard study on performance, experts found that the habit of being excellent—in other words, practicing the proper way to do something on a daily basis—was a greater factor in individual achievement than pure talent. If you want to become great, outshine your competition in the marketplace and create a remarkable life, practicing excellence is your answer.

Tip#3: Focus on your finish

Sometimes your goals can look gigantic, and it feels like success will take much longer than you planned. Each day, just remember to stay focused on the end result. See the outcome you desire from the very beginning. I create vision boards, review my Dream Book and have my success triggers handy to help me keep my success in sight. This way, I always have a clear view of what I'm working for. When you see where you want to be, it will help you stay motivated and keep moving. Never allow yourself to get overwhelmed; imagine yourself completing the task and accomplishing the goal. Stay focused on finishing, don't quit and eventually your daily efforts will produce the dream life you really want.

Take Fast Action

1. Write down one thing that you can do for 30 minutes each day that would really make a difference. What can you do daily to put you ahead of the game? Starting this week do that one thing you've written for 7 consecutive days. Then note your results in your journal. If are pleased with how that action has improved your productivity add it to your daily routine.

2. Make a list of 4 things you can do to add more excellence to your business and life. Over the next 30 days implement one thing on your list each week.

3. Starting in the morning, write down your top 3 goals. Then write at least one thing you will do before the day ends to reach those goals. Then take 5 minutes to imagine yourself completing the tasks and accomplishing your goals. Do this daily until you reach the goals then move on to the next set of goals.

SUCCESS ATTRACTION QUOTE NOTES:

I DECREE *I AM DILIGENT*

I DECREE:

I decree that I'm diligent in my efforts to succeed. My daily routines, habits and actions cause me to achieve and perform at top levels. I have the proper perspective and am willing to put in the work it takes to reach my goals. I am a finisher and I complete everything I do in excellence. I achieve the desires of my heart because I am willing to put in the work. I work hard and enjoy the fruits of my labor.

Journal Notes

Journal Notes

Success Note #20

ORDER
Always Precedes
INCREASE

Take 30 Minutes to Bring Order to One Area of Your Life Today

#20 Order Always Precedes Increase

Order makes life work—and it ultimately makes you more money. When you upgrade your surroundings by adding order, you will increase your productivity and enjoy your life more. The first step to abundance is cleanliness. Cleaning up creates a new direction. It opens the pathway for new opportunities to come shining through. Clutter speaks volumes to you and takes up mental space. Whether you are cleaning up your closet, your car, your refrigerator or your attitude, every time you put in the effort to clean up your life space, new opportunities will appear.

Get an atmosphere upgrade. Evaluate your décor, then de-clutter. Brighten your house with the proper lighting. Paint drab walls. De-clutter and get rid of anything hindering your creativity and ability to think clearly. Create clean, organized spaces where you can be productive, both at home and in the workplace. You will experience so much more peace and clarity. Once you've created an orderly environment, you've cleared the way for your money-making ideas to flow. Here are four quick ways to help you de-clutter and position yourself for increase.

1. Don't defeat yourself before you get started. The thought of de-cluttering your life may seem a bit overwhelming, but it is a lot easier than you think. Prepare yourself for the process by thinking positively. Take a few moments to sit quietly and imagine a clean, orderly home and office that is peaceful and beautifully decorated. Allow your mind and emotions to fully engage in this movie playing in your mind. Studies show you will attract what you consistently imagine. Next, make a plan and take action.

2. Focus on one task at a time. Don't create a task of epic proportions right from the start. Just take on one area at a time and complete it. Look around your home and workspace and decide what bothers you the most. What continually frustrates you? Is your closet in complete disarray? Does a Tupperware avalanche occur every time you open the cabinet? Is your desk a disaster? Choose one of the areas that disturb you daily and start there. Hone in on that one spot until it's completed, then move on.

3. Make de-cluttering a team effort. Inform and instruct your family regarding your de-cluttering efforts. If you are running a company, get your staff involved in your efforts. Explain thoroughly what you are doing and how you want them to help. Make it clear that you want the entire team to share the responsibility of upkeep after it's been de-cluttered, so that your efforts won't be in vain.

Encourage and inspire all those around you to make your living and work spaces a clutter-free zone. Once you've conquered the clutter, create a system and schedule to keep it that way. Even just 15 minutes before closing time or before bed each day can be enough to keep your spaces neat, tidy and welcoming. Practice this "conquer the clutter" routine on a daily basis and you will find yourself less stressed, less distracted and more able to focus and get the most important things done.

Adding order to your life brings peace of mind and leads to a bigger bottom line. Taking the time to organize your business and home will clear the clutter from your thinking in order to let those brilliant money-making ideas shine through.

Take Fast Action

1. Sit quietly for 10 minutes and imagine a clean, orderly, beautifully decorated home and office. Then grab your journal and write down a plan of action.

2. Look around your home and workspace and decide what bothers you the most. Then start with that area. Set a deadline by which you will have your first area de-cluttered and organized.

3. Create a "conquer the clutter" routine for your staff or family to follow on a daily basis and implement it within the next two weeks.

SUCCESS ATTRACTION QUOTE NOTES:

I DECREE *ORDER*

I DECREE:

I decree that my business and personal life are in order. I am positioned for great increase. My thought process is sharp and I am a master planner.

I fulfill all of my roles and responsibilities with ease and in excellence. I have the proper systems in place for me to prosper.

Journal Notes

Journal Notes

Success Note # 21

#21 Get Passionate About the Possibilities

If you really want to live an extraordinary life, you will have to vividly imagine your success, become passionate about all the possibilities, then begin to pursue your vision of what's possible. Life is so much richer when you become enthusiastic about your own passions and take action. When you are passionate about your own possibilities, people are more likely to get on board with your vision. Be fervent about your business aspirations, dreams and personal goals. Believe me, you have barely tapped into what you are capable of accomplishing. As you become more passionate, not only will you begin to attract more success, you will attract purpose partners, dream drivers and others who are put in place to help you succeed. Here are three ways to help you spark your passion about life's possibilities.

1. Plan purposefully. Begin your planning by taking time to discover what you love. To build a life that you enjoy, not only must you get passionate about the possibilities, you must pay attention to what feeds you and to what nourishes your soul.

Have you ever asked yourself this question: *"Am I currently doing what I want to spend the rest of my life doing?"* Can you see yourself progressing toward your ultimate goal? Or are you just working to provide food and shelter for yourself and your family?

Focus on what you have felt most satisfied doing, regardless of what others think or have said you should feel. Don't try to do everything. Focus on what you are good at. Expand and amplify your gifts. Hone the skills that you must have and stay focused on what will bring you success.

I want to help you discover what you love, beginning now, so take a moment to answer the following questions:
What is easy and effortless for me to do?
Am I ready to step out and do purpose?

Who am I meant to be at my highest level?
Have I ever really planned out my life and what it is supposed to look like?

Discovering the master plan for your life may not be as mysterious as you think. Your plans are revealed from people who cross your path, places that you travel to, and CDs that you listen to. That's why it's essential that you don't make decisions based on cost, but on the value that the purchase will provide.

2. Enjoy mind-expanding experiences. One of the best ways to get passionate about the possibilities is to expand your mind. To expand your mind you have to experience something new. When you find yourself getting stuck in a rut, it's time to shake things up and get out of your comfort zone. You will become more passionate about what is possible when you open up your mind to new experiences. Go on a mind-expanding experience. Go someplace new: a new city, a new store, a new restaurant. Experience culture: a museum, an art gallery or a play. Try a new activity, sport or game. While I have my favorite spots to shop and dine everywhere I go, I also love trying new and different places. The experience often sparks ideas and creativity for my next project. When I take the time for mind-expanding experiences, I'm able to learn something new and gain more exposure, which I can share with those I coach.

3. Don't allow your inner critic to hinder your possibility thinking. While getting passionate about the possibilities, don't allow your inner critic to get the best of you. It's that die-hard inner critic that causes you to look through distorted lenses at yourself and your dreams, supersizing every obstacle from a molehill into a mountain and shrinking you from a giant to a grasshopper. Disregard this voice. Allow yourself to hope, believe and dream again. You've got to know that you are on the way to becoming the best in the business and go after it with gusto. Re-ignite your passionate for what your future can hold. You are just one thought, one action, one person, one conversation, one day away from an amazing existence. Silence your inner critic and believe in yourself again! Become your own biggest cheerleader. Self-esteem and success go hand in hand.

Take Fast Action

1. Today answer the following questions in your journal:

What is easy and effortless for me to do?
Am I ready to step out and do purpose?
Who am I meant to be at my highest level?
Have I ever really planned out my life and what it is supposed to look like?

2. Make plans within the next 30 days to go someplace new: visit a new city, store, or restaurant. Experience culture: enjoy a museum, an art gallery or a play. Try a new activity, sport or game.

3. Become your own biggest cheerleader. Tonight in your journal write a list of 20 things that you love about yourself.

SUCCESS ATTRACTION QUOTE NOTES:

I DECREE *POSSIBILITIES*

I DECREE:

I decree that I am a success story in the making. My ideal life is manifesting more and more each day. I journalize about my dreams and goals and take the appropriate actions to see them come to pass. I am passionate about my life's possibilities and very grateful for every opportunity that comes my way.

Journal Notes

Journal Notes

Success Note #22

PREPARE

For an

OPPORTUNITY

that doesn't exist yet

Today Purchase One Success Tool That Will Help You to Achieve Your Goals

#22 Prepare For an Opportunity that Doesn't Exist Yet

Living a totally successful life begins with preparing for opportunities that don't exist—yet. If you want to realize your dreams and stay on the success track, you must prepare for the life you want. Preparation provokes opportunity your way. As you engage in the preparation process, you will begin to attract new people and new ideas, and usher in new relationships that can shift your life for the better. Here are a few tips to help you to keep preparing and pressing toward a lifetime of success.

1. Be informed. There are so many resources and technology available that can cause you to have success. I encourage you to prepare for an opportunity that doesn't exist yet. You have to get out and look for information. You can't sit at home in front of your computer all day long and think that everything will just drop into your lap. That's not how your dreams happen.

Become an avid reader. You must read if you want to succeed. Pick up magazines; use highlighters to mark information that you can use later. Find books in your field and read them. Stop letting great information collect dust. Carve out time in your day to learn new information. I often check out information apps on my phone when I'm on the go, to stay current and informed. This is how you prepare for an opportunity that doesn't exist yet. Doors of opportunity will open for you—make sure you prepare for them.

2. Be image-conscious. This is a great time to review your brand and see how the world sees you. Take a step back and do a complete overview of your brand. Find out what you look like to your clients, customers and prospects that visit your website and social media pages.

Check over your tweets and posts. What kind of pictures do your posts paint for yourself and your business? Determine where you need a makeover in your business. Then take a look in the mirror and examine your personal image. Ask yourself,

"Do I need to upgrade myself?" Where can you make a few tweaks to get yourself prepared for the next big break? What do you want to happen with your vision, goals and the direction of your business? Make sure your intentions and your brand image match. Your image tells others how you want to be approached. Set up your personal and corporate image so that people will begin to approach you and want to work with you.

3. Stay inspired. Entrepreneurs often become stuck and bogged down with all the responsibilities of building their business. If you're in a rut and looking for a way out of your current situation, or you need specific guidance in pursuing your purpose, don't give up on your dreams. Instead, stay inspired, keep pushing forward, and continue to prepare. Every year, women secure their spot at my Women's Success Conference to ensure that they receive the life- and mind-shifting inspiration they need. Throughout the year, I hear from the ladies who've attended the conference as they share how they have been inspired to impact the world by being the women they were meant to be. To prepare for opportunities that don't exist yet, you have to keep inspiration flowing in your life.

4. Work with what you have. One of the best ways to prepare for an opportunity that doesn't exist yet is to work with what you already have until you've exhausted all your resources. For example, if you are in a coaching program, have you really finished all the exercises and lessons? Have you followed through on sales leads that you already have? Have you completely cleaned your home in preparation for the new furniture you desire? Have you taken action on the advice you've already been given from highly successful others? Ask yourself, "What have I done with the information I already have?" Life doesn't really work until you do. Begin to do what you can with what you already have in your hands.

Take Fast Action

Pull out your journal tonight and answer the following questions:

1. Am I prepared for the success I desire?
If not, why?
2. What image adjustments do I need to make?
3. What can I do right now with what I already have?

SUCCESS ATTRACTION QUOTE NOTES:

I DECREE *I'M PREPARED*

I DECREE:

I decree that I am prepared for every opportunity that comes my way. I study to show myself approved, **sharpen my skills and increase my expertise every day. I purchase the success tools that help me to** achieve my goals. My image is top-notch. My appearance causes favor and creates opportunities for me. I stay inspired and informed so I'm ready to take action. I am so grateful that I've prepared myself for success so that I can maximize each day and blessing that comes my way.

Journal Notes

Journal Notes

Success Note #23

Read to Succeed

Today Get Away and Absorb a Great Book

#23 Read to Succeed

The habit of reading is absolutely life-changing. You can find the answers to difficult issues and information to help you through tough times in books, magazines, and other great materials. Take inventory of your life and pinpoint what you need to know to get where you want to go. My book, The Success Secrets of a Reader, explains this concept completely. Reading is so exciting because not only does it expand our knowledge base, but it also fuels our own ideas and creative work.

To make your reading experience more enjoyable, begin reading with curiosity, looking for new ideas. Find strategies you can instantly implement into your life. Write down action steps you can take from what you've learned. If you will begin to read with this kind of enthusiasm and energy, the task of reading will begin to be profoundly meaningful.
Begin the new discipline of reading. You will miss outstand-

ing opportunities because of a lack of knowledge if reading is not a part of your daily life. Mark Twain said it well, "The man who does not read good books, has no advantage over the man who can't read them." Make an investment in yourself and your future. Purchase learning materials, tapes, and especially books. Be aware of what they are worth to your lifestyle.

The practice of reading:
- *Enhances your creativity*
- *Boosts your vocabulary and knowledge of grammar*
- *Causes you to be a better thinker*
- *Makes you evaluate yourself*
- *Challenges you to make positive changes*
- *Expands your goals*
- *Increases your knowledge and awareness of the world*
- *Broadens your interests and satisfies your curiosity*
- *Ignites you to generate new ideas*

8 Ways to Sharpen Your Reading Skills:

1. **Set aside time each day** for silent reading of things that you are interested in.
2. **If you have trouble reading, get help!** Take some reading comprehension courses. Take an English class. Don't be afraid to go back to school or take a course! Hire yourself a tutor if necessary.
3. **Be curious about new words.** Get a dictionary and try to learn a word a month. The more you learn, the better a reader you will be.
4. **Be a take-charge reader**. Conquer reading a book that is a little difficult for you.
5. **Be aware of your level of understanding**. Wise people can identify where they really are, and do something about it.
6. **Visit the library.** Get yourself a library card. Spend a day researching a topic of interest.
7. **Keep track of the books you read in a reading log, a book report form, or in a journal**. I use my iPad so I have the information at my fingertips.

8. **Vary your reading.** Try magazines, biographies, poetry, dictionaries, or possibly a novel.

Reading has the power to make an immediate transformation in your life through brilliant truths and "aha!" moments. When you read, you tap into a reservoir of ideas for your purpose. Books, magazines and home study courses are often the very road maps to the next phase in our lives.

Take Fast Action

1. To-do today: Answer the following questions

Where are you headed today?

What books and programs do you need to get you where you really want to be?

What needs to be on your shelves in a hurry?

Give yourself a deadline to gather the new information you need right away.

I DECREE

I READ TO SUCCEED

I DECREE:

I decree that my habit of reading manifests riches in my life. I make time to get away and absorb a good book because I am an avid reader. I come across the perfect books and resources to provide the solutions, strategies and ideas I'm in need of right now. I easily and effortlessly grasp everything I read and understand how to apply it to my life and business for increase. I am so grateful that I have developed the daily habits to expand my mind and lead me to success.

Journal Notes

Journal Notes

Success Note # 24

SAY Something in the DIRECTION of your Dreams DAILY!

STOP and SPEAK 5 Great Things About Your Future Now.

#24 Say Something in the Direction of Your Dreams

Your words create your world. You can walk in what I call divine dominion if you just dare to dominate with your words. Once you change what you say to line up with your purpose, you can change your life's outcome. The entire universe is waiting for you to give it instructions. By purposefully and carefully using our words, we can call things right into existence! Take out your goals list and begin to declare your success.

For example, say, "I am a millionaire with a successful company." Speak in the present tense, like it has already happened. Keep saying it until you believe what you are saying in your heart and mind. Do this every day for the next 30 days and watch: You'll experience more abundance and success in 30 days than you have in the last three years.

Did you know for years that actors, athletes, salespeople and leaders from around the world have been using confessions and written affirmations to reach their goals? I've used this practice for years to create the results I have in my life and business. I have also taught my kids and clients to use this method to create their dream life.

One client shared at one of our live events how he wrote an affirmation and declared his way out of bankruptcy, and is now making more money that he has ever made in his life.

Another of my coaching course members described what kind of clients they wanted and how much they wanted to be paid in three months time, and it happened just like they said it would.

Every morning I speak positive things about my business and my life. I encourage you to do the same. Your life's outcome is directly affected by the words that come out of your mouth, so keep it positive.

Self-talk is powerful; be your own promoter. Say something

aloud daily that encourages you to push forward toward your desired goals.

Take time daily to confess the best over your life—it super-charges your beliefs! I have embedded positive affirmations in every area of my life. Daily, I take time to attract success with the words of my mouth.

Stop for a moment: Think about how you talk. During a normal day, how many positive things do you say? How many negative things? What kinds of things are you saying about your business ventures? What are you saying about your ability to earn money?

NOTE: Whatever you are saying on the inside, you are seeing in your life.

Your positive words signal to your brain and the world around you to go to work on getting good things done for you daily. I say good things about my life, my business, my money, my health and my relationships every day. It's a principle and a process that really works. Begin to decree your purpose and goals coming to pass. The entire universe is waiting for you to give it instructions. Success after success will start to happen once you successfully order your words.

Take Fast Action

Create a success affirmation

Here are a few quick easy tips to help you:

1. Take three areas that you want to improve in—visualize what you want and allow your senses to feel what you have imagined as if it has already happened; it's time to begin to make note of what you saw in your mind's eye.

2. Now, write a paragraph for each one stating the outcome you desire. Write the phrase like it has already happened. You could write something like, "I make massive money daily. I am a master at what I do, so millions of clients seek my services/ products every day. I have changed thousands of lives by becoming an expert in my field."

3. Be sure that your affirmations are very positive. For example, don't say, "I hate being broke and I won't be poor anymore." Instead say, "I will enjoy a full life of prosperity and abundance."

4. Once you have your three small paragraphs, say them daily. Sometimes I say my affirmations in front of my mirror for an extra boost to my confidence. This works! When you start saying the right things, you will see quite a change in your life.

SUCCESS ATTRACTION QUOTE NOTES:

I DECREE
& SPEAK SUCCESS

I DECREE:

I decree that of all of my dreams come to pass and I achieve my goals. My words are powerful. I use my words as a creative force. I respect the law of confession and only speak great things about my future. Every day I say something in the direction of my dreams and am grateful to experience such awesome results.

Journal Notes

Journal Notes

Success Note # 25

Sometimes You Just HAVE to Show-Up

List 5 Events You Must ATTEND THIS YEAR to ensure your SUCCESS. Take Action NOW to Secure Your Spot

#25 Sometimes You Just Have to Show Up

No matter who you are or what you are striving to become, in order to succeed, eventually you must show up wherever the information you need is being offered. People who go big in their business and achieve their dreams are the ones who have learned the secret to showing up. They show up at the right time for the right opportunities, and consequently increase the odds of succeeding in their favor.

I've found that one of the biggest reasons that people fail in business and often in life is because they lack the proper connections and access to the right information to succeed. They are facing many obstacles and setbacks that—without the right relationships—can be really hard to handle. The odds of going it alone are just not promising.

You need successful others to empower you to succeed. You

need success environments to ignite your creativity, expand your thinking and push you to try new things in your business. You need success connections to inspire you to go higher, keep going and never give up.

A big part of your success is connecting with others. You can't do that if you're hiding out at home, behind your computer … or holed up in your store, buried in paperwork … You have to get out, get connected and get going … there are people, places, and programs already positioned to help you manifest your greatest desires.

Business conferences, workshops and events can be the perfect environment for you to grow to the next level. Showing up to events increases your chances of connecting with the right person to help you take your business to the next level. Studies show that entrepreneurs that frequently associate with other business owners are more likely to have success in their businesses. Here are three reasons why you need to show up to an environment of success:

1. You can achieve your dreams, grow your business and live the life you truly desire when you show up. Showing up is about pushing past the obstacles, life circumstances, and any excuse that could be holding you back from being where you need to be to succeed. Showing up is a testament of your drive and ambition to succeed at all costs. Pushing past obstacles to show up in the right places builds fortitude and increases your chances of winning big in life by 80 percent.

2. When you show up, you get answers. In those times when you're frustrated or fatigued or worried about your business, and what was working for you is no longer producing good results, show up to an event, program or conference for answers. You will almost always discover that you are not alone; others have been where you are. You'll also learn that there's a better way to solve your problem. You may have heard the saying, "Can't see the forest, for the trees."

A common phrase which simply means you are missing the big picture because your focusing on the smaller thing. Showing up at a conference can give you the BIG perspective so you can see a better way of reaching your goals. Lastly, you'll discover a continual source of inspiration to keep you on track long-term. When you come across an irresistible offer to connect with a coach or mentor long-term, jump in! Especially when you've been with them for a few days and you know your life changed from being there. That's just a great indicator of what's to come when you connect long-term.

3. When you show up, you get connected. There are other successful people just like you. They are your co-creators, dream drivers and purpose partners, and they are all waiting to connect with you. Under any other circumstance, you may never share the same air with some of the people you meet at events. You can easily develop relationships with like-minded entrepreneurs and business leaders that support you and will partner with you to grow your business. One year at my conference, we had a lady hire her stylist right on the spot, so another business owner closed a $3,000 deal over dinner. This is what you can expect when you are surrounded by like-minded leaders and business owners coming together. Purposeful and profitable relationships and opportunities come about when you show up.

Showing up in the right places at the right time is very transformative. It's the difference between the successful and the want-to-be successful. See, the successful always show up against the odds. No matter what the circumstance, they let nothing get in their way of a divine appointment. Once they get a witness that they are supposed to get on board, nothing can stop them.

Take Fast Action

Write a list of places you need to show up to. Then list all the benefits of showing up to each place. What connections can you make? What information will you learn and what answers will you get?

SUCCESS ATTRACTION QUOTE NOTES:

I DECREE *I ALWAYS SHOW UP*

I DECREE:

I decree that I always show up for my divine appointments. I connect to my purpose partners and all those put in place to ensure my success. I attend the right events and connect with the right people. I always have the finances to show up wherever I'm supposed to be. I am so grateful that because of my efforts to always show up, I have great favor wherever I go.

Journal Notes

Journal Notes

Success Note #26

Successful People

Leave Clues

Set Up a Meeting with a Mentor Or Enlist a Coach Today!

#26 Successful People Leave Clues

While on the success track, you don't have to waste time reinventing the wheel, because successful people leave clues. All you need to do is find the right person to follow. When striving to reach your dreams and goals, you can't be afraid to follow the leader. The fastest way to get somewhere in life is to connect with and follow the path of someone who has already been where you want to go.

Expand your connections and begin to associate higher. Get into circles of people who are achieving great things. Begin with your current acquaintances, and expand from there. It's OK to be a little intimidated by those who are very successful, but don't let that stop you from reaching out to them. Invite someone who is an expert in your field out for lunch or coffee. Be armed and ready with questions, and then be quiet and listen. Soak up their wisdom and make sure to express your appreciation for their time.

Besides building your network with successful others, seek out a mentor or coach to help fast-forward your success. Doing so can be vital to your personal and professional success. A coach can give you insight, ideas, strategies and action steps to ensure you reach your highest potential. They can provide guidance, clarity, wisdom and direction. If people who are at the top in their industries keep themselves accountable to a coach, then it's time you think about doing the same. A great coach will take you farther than you can take yourself alone.

Take Fast Action

Answer the following questions in your journal:

1. In what areas in my life do I need mentorship?
2. Where am I stuck in my business or personal life?
3. What action will I take this week to connect to a coach that can fast track my success?

I DECREE

I FOLLOW SUCCESSFUL OTHERS

I DECREE:

I decree that I always enlist the perfect mentors, coaches and follow those who have **a proven track record of success. I have a teachable attitude and pick up on all** clues left by successful others. I practice the principles I learn from them and enjoy great results. I always win. I connect to and adopt the habits and practices of winners.

Journal Notes

Journal Notes

Success Note #27

Start A Change Campaign. Make One Personal Adjustment EVERY day for the Next 30 Days

#27 Take an Active Role to Change Whatever Isn't Best About You

It's time for a change campaign! So many people go through life tolerating their shortcomings, faults and bad habits—the very things holding them back from what they want most: a successful life. If you want to accomplish great things in life, you have to get mentally tough and take an active role to change whatever isn't best about you. Most of us are quite aware of the areas in which we are lagging. For the record, though, stop and take a few moments right now and list the self-improvements you know you must make. What changes have you been longing to make? What have been the hang-ups you have had in the past? What's been your one vice? Write them down ... but whatever the issue, you don't have to stay stuck here.

You can reinvent yourself and your life if you are truly committed to the process. I am going to share with you five simple keys to creating a new you. Here are three steps to creating your change campaign!

1. Ponder: Take time for self-reflection and self-evaluation. Creating a new you begins with doing a reflective examination of yourself. What habits do you need to change? What old habits will you let go of and what new habits will you form so you can be more successful? In what areas do you fall short? How can you ensure that doesn't happen again? You have to make an internal decision once and for all to be your best self. Learn from the mistakes of the past, and then let them go.

2. Plan: Write your vision for a new you. Make a list of all of your goals—everything you want to accomplish, see, experience, acquire and become. Don't limit yourself. Write down everything that comes to mind. Challenge yourself to think bigger. Don't downsize your goals; instead, upsize them.

Now, review your list and begin to plan it out. Even if you don't have the means to make everything happen immediately, plan for it. For example, if you desire to take a trip to Hawaii, look at the calendar and choose a month to go. Do as much preliminary planning as you can for each of your goals. Act as if things are happening for you right now!

3. Push yourself: Change now. Determine that you will push yourself for change right now and keep pressing until you meet all of your goals. Act fast, and act daily. Take action every day in a new way. Do something productive each day. Your success will depend on how fast you act. It is the key to continual results and greater success. Don't wait for the perfect conditions to make changes, but implement new information and ideas as quickly as possible. Commit to this process and don't look back!

Take Fast Action

Write your Dream Big Life List: Make a list of all of your goals—everything you want to accomplish, see, experience, acquire and become.

Take action in 48 hours. Make a phone call, book a reservation, take at least three actions in the next 48 hours to draw you closer to your dreams.

Keep taking action daily. Your momentum will increase as you continue to move. Soon you will become unstoppable!

I DECREE *CHANGE FOR THE BEST*

I DECREE:

I decree that I am diligent about change. I take an active role to upgrade myself until I am operating at my best. I routinely make the personal adjustments necessary to achieve my dreams and goals. I'm so grateful that my self-improvement practices continue to attract great levels of success in my life.

Journal Notes

Journal Notes

Success Note # 28

Become a

Trailblazer

In Your Own

Life!

Take Time Today to Learn and Do Something NEW!

#28 Become a Trailblazer in Your Own Life

To position yourself for lifelong success, you must continually reinvent yourself and refresh your thinking in order to stay relevant to the world around you. In short, you have to become a trailblazer in your own life; navigating fresh new paths to the dream life you desire. This requires a new approach to your life and business. To become a trailblazer in your own life you have to do something new—take new actions, acquire a new perspective, learn a new skill ... and the list goes on. The following keys will help you put a new spin on how you normally operate, and blaze your way to bigger profits and a better way of life.

1. Start before you're ready. Don't wait until everything is lined up perfectly. It'll never happen. There are no perfect conditions. If you want to get something done, you have to just start. Start when you get the idea and you know that this is something you are supposed to do. Go ahead and start your book!

2. Stop second-guessing yourself. Many times you may experience resistance when you decide to improve your life and come up to another level. You may buy a new program or register for an event and then start thinking about whether you made the right decision. You start second-guessing yourself and conversing with the naysayers who don't understand the decision you made. They just want you to stay like them. Turn off the critics and know that if you are going to advance in life you must make an investment.

3. See it in your mind's eye. I believe you have to see it and believe it before you manifest it. Sometimes it's good to think and meditate about your vision and goals before sharing them with others. Spend time in the morning meditating on how you want the outcome to be. Dream big. This winning combination of steps will help you to blaze your own path to unlimited success.

Take Fast Action

Write down one thing that you can start before you're ready. Do you need to write a chapter in your book this weekend? Should you design and sew a new piece for your new clothing line? Where have you allowed procrastination to delay your dreams? Write it down and commit to getting started before the end of this week!

SUCCESS ATTRACTION QUOTE NOTES:

I
DECREE
I AM A
TRAILBLAZER

I DECREE:

I decree that I am a trailblazer in my industry. I creatively market my products and services, and it causes me to profit. I always make time to learn how to do new things that keep me ahead of my competitors. I never make excuses. I make money easily, and I always find a way to get things done.

Journal Notes

Journal Notes

Success Note # 29

YOU were *SELECTED* for Something SIGNIFICANT!

Today List 20 things You LOVE about You, and 20 Things YOU LOVE TO DO

#29 You Were Selected for Something Significant

You were selected for something significant so you don't want to waste a minute of your very precious life. To make the most of your time and ensure success, you must have a carefully crafted life plan. I often say that a successful life is woven together with care. There are many different ingredients that you must blend together to create an enjoyable lifestyle, but they all should be anchored on your purpose. What were you selected to do? Your unique assignment should direct you on your daily path.

Everything I do is to help other women enjoy life. I am called to motivate women and to teach them how to reach their greatest potential. Even the fun things that I enjoy are closely related to my purpose. What are you called to do?

One of the ways you can get clarity on your life's purpose is learning to recognize your internal cues and external clues.

External clues are hints from your surroundings that lead you toward purpose. They are things that you are drawn to like certain colors, styles, or activities that you enjoy. My signature colors are fuchsia, yellow, orange and green. I love to splash these vibrant hues anywhere I can to brighten up the atmosphere.

I favor very modern styles in art, furniture and architecture. When I evaluate the external things that I enjoy, it denotes my personal style of coaching. As I coach women, I want to brighten their lives and add giant splashes of color. With every product, conference, seminar and book, I try to present timeless principles of success in a very new and modern way. My external clues always provide inspiration and little suggestions to keep me focused on my purpose.

Internal cues are directives that come from the innermost part of you, and they provide suggestions and hints as to what you're called to do. It's that still, small voice that whispers a life-changing thought. Guidance from prayer, journalizing, and making notes of your passions are the inner cues that lead you to purpose.

As you discover more of your purpose and hone in on what you are passionate about, you will also discover where your profitability lies. Clarity leads to abundance. Please note that understanding your purpose and creating clearly defined goals does not mean you will not encounter road blocks to your dreams.

However, plugging in to the belief that you've been selected for something significant will strengthen your confidence and help you become unstoppable. You are talented, gifted and skilled with the incredible ability to attract the income and life that you truly desire.

Take Fast Action

1. Write down what you believe you are called to do in 3 sentences or less (If you are clear on what your purpose is, you can write it succinctly).

2. If you are not completely sure, **write a list of external clues and Internal cues in your journal tonight.**

3. If you haven't already done so, sign up for my free six-week Path 2 Purpose course at my Life Coach to Women site: ***www.Lifecoach2women.com***

I DECREE *SIGNIFICANCE*

I DECREE:

I decree that my life matters. I am selected for something significant. I have discovered my life's purpose and work actively each day to fulfill my greatest potential.

Journal Notes

Journal Notes

Success Note # 30

#30 What's Written is Real

One of the most powerful habits you can adopt on your road to success is the habit of writing things down. Writing is the foundation of all wealth. Writing clarifies. Writing solidifies. Writing organizes. I plan out every aspect of my life on paper—from listing what I need to get done the next day to writing down the wardrobe items I need to purchase for upcoming events or projects, my life is written and planned. You don't have to be a world-renowned strategist to develop some simple written systems to keep your life on track. When coaching my clients I always suggest they:

1.) Keep a calendar to list all the important dates for the year, that pertain to your life's priorities. Include birthdays and anniversaries of your family, friends and VIP relationships. Then add the dates of your family vacations and school functions.

Also add your important business and project deadlines as well as financial payment due dates. Once your priorities are scheduled, when other things crop up you will be able to use your calendar to see whether it fits with your life flow.

2.) Keep a "to-done" list. For years, I've advocated keeping a to-do list, but I've realized it's not what you are doing, but what you are getting ***done*** that counts. Write a list of what you will tackle and finish to completion the following day. This helps you prioritize your time more realistically and be more serious about your work. I try to list only three-five things that I absolutely will get done the next day and then I don't let anything stop me from achieving those main objectives. I may not always accomplish more than those things listed, but I never accomplish less. This list keeps my life and day moving forward.

3.) Write in your journal. Keeping a journal is an excellent way to avoid losing all the marvelous ideas that your creative mind is capable of churning out. I journalize daily in beautiful, pink journals. On these pages I write my life's story as I see it unfolding and strategize my next move.

You can literally write your way to success. Use your journal to record information, ideas and instructions from a course you're taking or books you're reading. Oftentimes when you are learning new information, your mind is flooded with new ideas and things you can implement in your life and business. Write those thoughts in your journal so you can have a catalog of strategies to build from. Several students from my 37 Journaling Secrets Course used this method to expand their business with new products and programs. Recording your thoughts and developing them is a very important key strategy in personal growth and always leads to more increase!

Take Fast Action

Here are three ways that you should add writing to your lifestyle:

1. Create a Writing Routine

Do it daily. One of the most powerful practices you partake in to have super success is daily journaling. Daily journaling has a significant affect on what you accomplish every day...and even your mood! Your journal will give you laser like focus on what is working in your life and business. That's what makes it a super powerful tool! If you are tech savvy, you can keep your journal on your computer or iphone.

Just be sure to use a medium where you can:

- Keep records of what you write
- Offers the least amount of resistance
- Yet has a great amount of visibility to you!

2. Write Your Goals Daily

When your goals are written down on paper, they become inscribed in your mind! Write down your goals and then rewrite them daily. They will ultimately and inevitably show up in your future! Goals are a preview for future events and experiences in your life!

3. Write a Nightly Gratitude List

Before you go to bed tonight, I want you to place your

journal and pen next to your bed. Write your entry date at the top of your page and then begin to write as many things that you can think of that you are grateful for! Let your gratitude flow! Writing what you are grateful for increases your happiness by as much as 25%. Plus, it attracts more success into your life to be grateful for!

After you do this exercise the first time, continue on by writing a gratitude list nightly before you go to bed. Take a few minutes each night to pull out your journal and list 10 or more things that you can say made your day an amazing day, regardless of circumstances. Thankfulness always puts in motion more good things to come your way. Close your night with a heart full of gratitude and you will generate days full of goodness! What's written is real. Create a new and improved reality with your pen and paper!

SUCCESS ATTRACTION QUOTE NOTES:

I DECREE *I WRITE MY WAY TO SUCCESS*

I DECREE:

I decree that I write my way to success. My written goals become inscribed in my mind and manifest in my life. I write the right things daily and pen my own success story. My future is bright because what I've written is real!

Journal Notes

Journal Notes

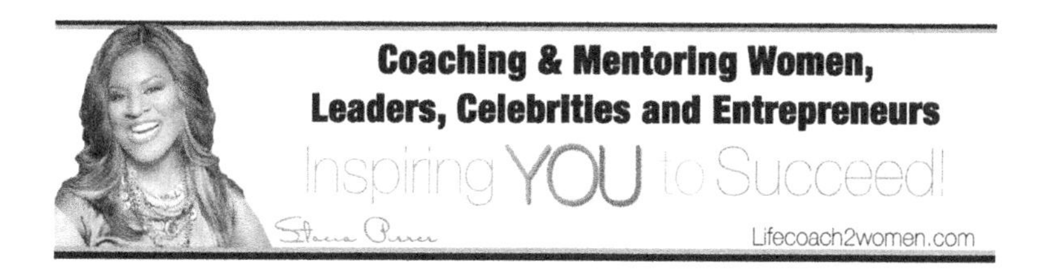

Stacia Pierce Award-Winning Life Coach Motivational Speaker & Entrepreneur

When you first get a glimpse of what a single day in the life of Stacia Pierce entails, you begin to wonder if she somehow has more than 24 hours in her day. Your first encounter with this award-winning Life Coach is guaranteed to be a whirlwind of passion, excitement and motivation bundled up into a highly-acclaimed business woman, paving the way for the limitless success of her clients.

With a contagious energy and an impressive roster of motivational and entrepreneurial successes, LifeCoach2Women.com Founder and CEO Stacia Pierce has taken empowerment to an entirely new level by helping others turn obstacles into opportunities.

A living example of success, Pierce was named Top Women Who Mean Business by the Orlando Business Journal for her system of turning passions into paychecks, enabling her to motivate fellow entrepreneurs worldwide. Pierce has worked with everyone from the Hollywood elite, to Grammy- and Emmy-winners, to television personalities, several successful business owners, lawyers, doctors and government officials throughout the United States, Canada, and the Bahamas.

Her 'No Excuses' business philosophy encourages clients to take responsibility for every aspect of their lives and businesses. Pierce has also developed her highly-acclaimed 'Success Attractions Strategies', a vast collection of success tools, seminars and conferences triggering exploration of self-creativity, while embracing the possibilities of a better, more fulfilling and healthier way of life.

And it doesn't stop there! Pierce also created several additional success tools to encourage the adaptation of reaching your highest potential. Dubbed a 'Whole Life Coach', she has mastered the art of overhauling the lives of clients, leading them to discover their true selves, as well as their true potential.

With the use of straight-to-the-point, candid stories and highly-charged anecdotes, she inspires people to find their inner 'Dream Driver'. Regardless of the goal, Pierce focuses her unwavering dedication to empower women to freely and smartly chase their greatest desires with confidence and knowledge.

Her educational successes are equally impressive having earned a Doctorate of Philosophy and Religious Studies from Friends International University, as well as a Doctorate of Divinity from St. Thomas College. Outstanding community service projects like the Women Caring for Women event, and the entrepreneur economic improvement program's Shop and Swap Professional Empowerment event, have earned her additional honors.

With books, newsletters, retail products, appearances and countless online outlets as part of her growing empire, Pierce is able to inspire over 100,000 people weekly and shows no signs of slowing down.

FOLLOW STACIA FOR COACHING SUCCESS TIPS AND INSPIRATION

"Information changes the seasons of your life."

For more of my success tips and business to-do's Scan below to visit my website

Get Tag Reader free mobile APP for your phone at http:gettag.mobi Then SCAN the STACIA TAG to the left with your Smartphone to learn more about Stacia Pierce

Stacia Pierce
imagine. improve. increase.
Ultimate Lifestyle Enterprises, LLC

Lifecoach2women.com

Made in the USA
Monee, IL
05 November 2020